GENTLEMAN APPROACH

GENTLEMAN APPROACH

HOW BEING A GENTLEMAN WILL SECURE YOUR SUCCESS

W.M. ESTES

Charleston, SC
www.PalmettoPublishing.com

Gentleman Approach
Copyright © 2023 by W. M. Estes

All rights reserved
No portion of this book may be reproduced, stored in a retrieval system, or transmitted in any form by any means–electronic, mechanical, photocopy, recording, or other–except for brief quotations in printed reviews, without prior permission of the author.

First Edition

Paperback ISBN: 979-8-8229-1644-9

A GUIDE FOR DEVELOPING TRUE RELATIONSHIPS

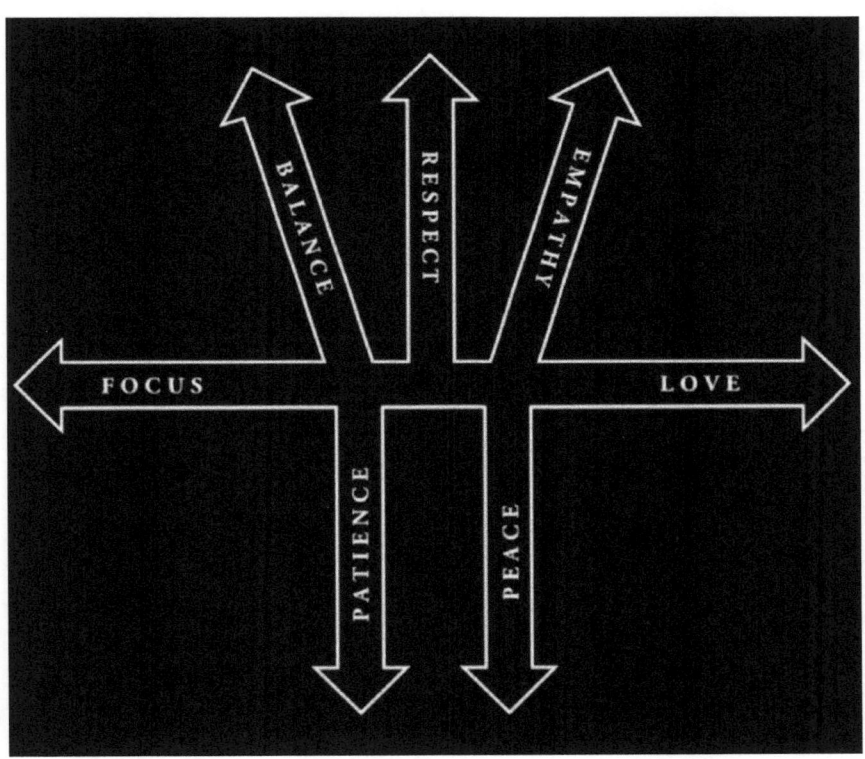

DEDICATION

Dedicated to my mother for always being my rock … and my brothers and sisters for having my back, no matter the circumstances.

Thank you always.

TABLE OF CONTENTS

Introduction..xi

Chapter 1: Establish Yourself..1

Chapter 2: Become One With All Things...................14

Chapter 3: Harness Your Inner Voice.......................22

Chapter 4: How to be on Standby............................30

Chapter 5: Embrace the Silence..............................38

Chapter 6: Have Open Arms...................................46

Chapter 7: Take Time to Understand.......................53

INTRODUCTION

As you explore this journey, I invite you to open your mind while experiencing different aspects of life through a new lens. You will develop tactful ways to combat obstacles that may arise in your path while maintaining your respect and dignity. You will come to realize that the gentleman's approach—with a firm grasp on what really matters in life—will enhance your way of living, making it more productive and gratifying. It ultimately will give you a sense of purpose.

The basis of this book is to create and sustain a more authentic type of man in our world today. I believe that most men in this day and age have neglected the responsibility of what it means to be a good man. My goal is to help restore the traits of men they were created for but have been long forgotten.

Society has put its set of standards on what it means to be a man in today's world. They tell you to concentrate on the exterior rather than the interior, which couldn't be further from the truth. The foundation is the most essential part of the structure as it is what is inside that is so important and really makes you who you are. The part that's rarely seen but holds everything in place; it's a good place to start.

I will be breaking down 7 keywords in their purest form that all can relate to. You will adopt a keen sense of depth and understanding as you read each one. I give a series of scenarios that you can analyze. These will be everyday situations that most of us have encountered or will in the future.

Let yourself be transformed and changed for the better by these well-thought-out and time-tested, real-life lessons, starting from the first page to the very last page of this book. You'll learn how to be a gentleman without compromising your own set of high standards. Be a warrior for doing the right thing while promoting good. Live your life like it's a requirement to be this way; make it who you are at your core. Become a beacon of hope that men would aspire to be. Reflect the change you want to see in others. Be the lighthouse that helps guide your fellow man in the right direction, because when you help your fellow man, your own life is elevated. I hope you find this information useful and hear clearly that ring of truth echoed in each sentence you read.

CHAPTER 1

ESTABLISH YOURSELF

Respect: to demonstrate high regard for or special attention to something or someone.

At the beginning of creating the man you want to be, there has to be respect. The standards you set for yourself should align with the person you want to become. These guidelines should influence every aspect of your life. They will be there for your protection and give you clear direction. This will keep you from going off course when situations arise that could derail you.

Having a full understanding of who you are is essential. You need to know who you really are and what you stand for before you can set standards and guidelines for success. Because what glitters isn't always gold and you may have some underlying issues not yet addressed within yourself that need attention, start there—taking a thorough look at your own infrastructure or foundation. Look at what's inside. You must start from the ground up, zero in and take a close look at the inner person. This will take some time. Don't take on too much all at once, so that you can't complete what you start. A little at a time; giving close attention to every aspect of yourself and the kind of person you want to be will have a huge impact on the person you become. This process should not be rushed to get the best results.

Establish your foundation and by no means let anyone interfere with this process. Evaluate your relationships, if those around you don't respect you enough to allow this growth to take place, then you don't need them around during this process. Especially if what they bring is negative or toxic. This is something that is not easy to hear but needs to be said, and more importantly, needs to be done. This will ensure that this important process of self-discovery will not be altered by anyone else's influence and ideas; the changes you make will be your own. Having a healthy knowledge of one's self is over half the battle of maintaining your self-respect and dignity through all situations unscathed.

Now that you have looked inward, let's take a look outward at other people you may encounter. When it comes to dealing with people, try keeping people at a distance until you understand them. Doing this will keep you from being caught off guard and possibly getting hurt in people's illegitimate attempts at getting too familiar. Sometimes, when you give people an inch, they may try and take a mile, taking full advantage of your generosity and becoming too familiar too fast. People in this category are not too hard to recognize. There are usually subtle signs. For example, when you open the door for certain people, they may take it one step further and kick off the hinges, trying to move right in with their feet propped up on the table. And you're left standing there in such disbelief, trying to figure out what just happened. Your journey is a personal process—learn the things that you like and the things you don't like—so whenever you come across people doing either one, you will be able to observe them to see if you want to engage or disengage. Pay attention to how you react in every situation and learn from it to improve yourself—become familiar with your weaknesses and your strengths.

Everyone doesn't have to know about the specifics—your personal mindset—but they do have to respect your space. Guarding your personal space will cause people to approach you differently, respectfully, and with caution. You will be putting a guard up for yourself that protects you from people with ill-gotten motives.

As you start to establish the man you want to be, you will see that this is the way you want to be and have to be, to remain at peace with who you are. Being true to yourself is most beneficial for your growth. Telling yourself inaccurate information just to make yourself feel better is only hindering your growth and is a waste of time.

Keep nonsense out of your life if you can; this will be helpful for your overall well-being. It would be wise to make a list of people or things in your life you may need to part ways with. If these people or things are more negative than positive, you may need to take steps to clean house; this is about bettering yourself, not settling. People may seem like their intentions are good, but most don't understand who they are, or what they stand for in life. You should hope for the best in people, but don't be surprised if you get their worst.

By setting and maintaining healthy boundaries, you can avoid future events before they arise. When you create these boundaries, it will allow you to see who they really are as people before you get too involved with them.

Once you realize what it is you stand for and what you won't stand for, it will get easier to filter out the type of people you want around and the ones you want nothing to do with. By putting your self-respect above everything else, you will be holding yourself to a healthy standard. No one will be able to penetrate this respect and the standards that you have placed upon yourself.

There will be people who feel like you think you're better than they are, and the simple truth is, they're right. Because you choose to be better, they have a choice just like you, and they made theirs—not to be better. Holding yourself to a higher standard is increasing your ability to be a better man. The only reason I say that is because if a person doesn't have respect for others or themselves, it becomes obvious—doesn't it? There are levels in life, and everyone isn't on the same one; it's time to be a realist. This information is for anyone who wants it. But not everyone does, some people are perfectly fine being dysfunctional and complacent. So, the ones who do want this information are most likely the type of people you would like to engage. That's not to say that we all have to be alike, but I do say that our core values should align for the most part. The issue isn't about being better than someone; it's about being a better you. The competition should be with yourself—no one else. You are trying to be better than you were; that's the goal. Let no one get in the way of that. You have a lot of people that don't respect themselves, so they feel it's fine to influence you to do the same. They don't want to improve, so they don't want you to improve. Become independent, learn to depend on yourself, and use the knowledge you have obtained. When it comes to being secure in yourself and who you are, that is what will get you through any situation. It's everything you need to be truly happy; it already resides within you. You just have to retrieve it; to activate it, you have to seek the things you need first, then the things you want will follow.

Learn to respect everyone even if they don't agree with you. You can still have a relationship in the end if you have some sense of understanding each other. Understanding yourself is foremost; once you have that down, you can be clearer on what and who you are. Standards form the person and keep them level-headed at all times—no matter the location or who's around.

Learn to be content with who you've become. Having a firm grip on the reality of the situation and who you are will develop a profound respect for yourself by others. This will positively affect them, making them want to change for the better—maybe even into the person they now see in you. It will make them think perhaps in a new way.

Doing the right thing isn't always easy, but it is necessary to remain in good standing with a healthy morale—the only way to be better is by doing better. Show your worth in your words and actions. Always speak positive. There is so much negative in the world; we need more people doing good in every way they can. Being liked by people doesn't have to jeopardize who you are so that people will accept you. By remaining true to who you are, you are building a wall between what's real and true and what's not. The goal isn't perfection, but progression. Try to make some changes in your life and do what you have to in order to obtain some of these goals that you are trying to reach. Evaluate your goals to make sure they're good for you overall. Let's reiterate; that we are not looking for perfection but progression in one's actions—break bad habits—so that you can re-establish yourself and be the man you want to be. These goals are reachable; you have to put forth the effort to get what it is you want. Visualize yourself completing all your goals. Now, plan to see it through and remember to be respectful in every way possible. By being this way, you will see that people will start to look at you as a man that has respect for himself and others.

Even if the entire society was to live without having this respect, you would still want to be this way—set your own standards and stick to them no matter what. Let people see that truth and self-respect will stand the test of time; once you incorporate this into your life, it will become part of who you are. Protect it with all your might. This is the most sacred thing you have that's truly yours. You will carry the torch of truth to everyone you come in contact with. This movement will become a new way of life. Instead of destroying yourself with the world's filth and junk that doesn't nourish your body, you'll be replenishing yourself with the nectar of life's principles. This way of living will ensure that your values and principles that were handed down to you by your creator will align. We have to be what our creator intended for us to be—representatives of him. The one that gave us life and equipped us with everything we need to succeed. Everything, in the end, goes right back to the one who gave it to us. Once you have a better understanding of that truth and apply it in your life, your life will only improve. You will also be able to help others by your own good example. The ground rules need to be laid out—providing guidance—then review them; be true to them and apply them throughout your life. These rules can be similar to the ten commandments in the bible, so create rules that can follow the structure and intentions of our heavenly father.

In order to establish who you are, you need to evaluate yourself, look at yourself in the mirror, and say who am I? When you ask this question, you're wanting to know who you are as a person and what you represent.

You should focus on the interior; the exterior is also important to some degree. But our main focus is to put more time and energy into the inner person. This is character building—the start of your core foundation. The inside is more important than the exterior because once age takes its toll on the physical body, it is the inside that can actually improve with age. By developing a respectable person within, the inner person will stand the test of time.

Reflect the qualities you want to see in others. Take a few deep breaths, then repeat these words, "I can do this;" "I can become a better man." With a little dedication and willpower, you can achieve innumerable things in your life. You will be the one who people respect and want to emulate. For you to change people, you must first change yourself where change is needed. Then you will help others make the changes they need as well. Put yourself first, learn yourself all the way, through and through. Your likes and dislikes, and once you have a full grasp of the things that matter to you and ignite or excite you, you can grow as a person.

Avoid situations that trigger your dislikes. This will keep your stress level down. Which in turn will allow you to think clearly and make sound decisions. Some stress is not always avoidable, but learn how to read into these situations so that you can pinpoint potential problems before they arise. This will help you avoid them and redirect the course of action to a more positive outcome.

Then when you realize what things really upset you, test yourself by putting yourself in these situations temporarily to improve your self-control during these situations. This is difficult to do, but it can be done successfully. You can't control all situations, but the one thing you can always control is the way you react and how you respond. No one can take this away from you as long as you're on this beautiful earth created for you and I. Once you start learning to control your emotions and impulses, you can develop peaceful energy even when your surroundings are unpleasant. You can create peace within, even in the chaos. This does take a lot of attention to detail, and by dedicating your time and energy towards becoming a more respectable gentleman, you can achieve these goals. This doesn't mean that you won't get upset when something happens. It's just finding an alternate outlet to redirect energy. Because things are going to happen, the way you respond to things makes all the difference. How you respond is going to affect you. And it's not going to change the event that already took place, but your response can change the entire outcome.

So, instead of being outraged at first, hold your words and thoughts until you can calm down a bit to get a grip on the situation. Think of it as a relief valve for your body. So, by releasing pressure in a creative healthier way, you will keep from overreacting and losing control, which in turn wouldn't be a good outcome.

By focusing on keeping calm and diffusing the situation, it will allow you to become aware of it and deflect it before it gets out of hand. Creative ways to decrease stress can be a real lifesaver at times. Here are a few ideas that help me during stressful times. (1) Exercise—this is primary for your mental health. It's also an alternative to medication. (2) Meditation—find time in your daily life to practice this. This mental escape can help heal your mind and give your brain a rest from the daily struggles of this world. (3) Breathing exercises for about 10 minutes—breathing in through your nose and exhaling through your mouth. This exercise will regulate your heart rate so that it's at a steady pace. Bringing your stress level down will calm you down when you're feeling high-strung. These are the go-to things that work for me regularly.

If you have other means that work for you, then use them—just find what works for you and don't forget to use them when you need to. So, when you need them, they will be there at a moment's notice. This is essential for your well-being; putting your mental health first is key to a healthy life. A sharp mind is more productive and influential. Write down a list of all unhealthy habits you have and work every day to get rid of those; this will help promote healthy living along with good decision-making skills. This is not always the easiest task to do, but it is important for moving forward. Take it one day at a time, start with one habit at a time, give yourself ample time to get rid of, or curve your desire for this habit you want to change before moving on to the next one. Don't worry about messing up or not getting it right the first time around. You are not going to change at a moment's notice; change takes time. But with a little determination, you'll be surprised what you will be able to accomplish.

You don't have to make a public announcement about the things you're working on. This will prevent any unwanted judgment from anyone that might have something discouraging to say. There's always someone with an opinion about something. Allow yourself to settle in with this task of rebranding yourself; the only judgment will come from you, which could also be damaging if you're too hard on yourself and not balanced. Don't get down on yourself about not getting things right on the first try. The process is about having an understanding of what you're trying to achieve.

Just imagine this project as a garden that you're planting. Except you're the garden, and what you put in it is exactly what you will get out of it. It takes cultivating to keep the garden up to date, so plant the seeds and watch the progression sprout. You are worth it; remember, no one can do this for you except you so let's get to work. It truly starts within, then eventually comes out for all to see. Remind yourself that you can do this, and you can. We're all capable of doing amazingly creative things; even starting with just a little power, we can grow from there.

Focus on how to be better about all things that are in your day-to-day life. You will find that the more you think positive thoughts, the more peaceful your days will be. You will start looking for positive situations and how to be more positive in everything you do. One day at a time, little by little, you will find it easier to do. It does require effort, but anything worth having, is worth working hard for.

Your body is your temple, and you need to treat it as such. Watch what you put in your temple because whatever you put in; you will surely get out. Positive thoughts beget positive results as negative thoughts beget negative results.

Take care of your mind and body; try eating healthy most of the time. What you eat affects how you feel, so if you're not feeling 100%, it could be because your diet is lacking and needs adjusting.

Also, incorporate a weekly exercise routine for at least 3 to 5 days a week. These exercises can be as simple as walking for 30 minutes a day, 5 times a week. A couple of exercises that would work are 5 sets of 25 push-ups, 5 sets of 20 squats, along with 5 sets of 10 dips, with stretching before and after workouts to prevent injury pre-workout or post-workout. But keep in mind that it's better to stretch warm muscles to prevent injury, so warm up first. These workouts I use throughout the week to maintain a healthy system of active cardio. It's good to be fit; you feel better when you look better. But don't let it go to your head, stay humble. A little active training goes a long way, but don't lose focus on your overall goals. It's a package deal you're working with. The whole body needs to be in alignment, not just the exterior but the interior also. It all works together to provide a balanced well-tuned machine.

Finding ways to test your growth after a certain amount of time would allow you to endure unpleasant situations and see your own progress. This will be a tolerance builder for things that annoy you, and learning to be silent in certain situations can be useful. When people see that you're annoyed, they may try to annoy you even more at times. So, not responding verbally will take tension off what they're doing or trying to do. To put it simply, what I'm saying is just ignore them. By not feeding the negative energy, it doesn't have a chance to grow. Destroy it at the source, so it doesn't evolve. These tips do work—I use them daily, and once you know firsthand how they work, you will start to see that they will help smooth out negative situations. As you continue to grow as a person, you will learn more productive alternative ways to address any issue, making the conscious choice not to respond negatively. This will allow you to stay in control and shine through to others in a positive way.

Creating a relationship with God is also a must. You are rebuilding your foundation, so He needs to be at the center of it, and because without Him, there is no you since He is your creator and life-giver.

Weekly bible studies are truly refreshing for one's spirit. Reading the bible daily is also beneficial. We can tend to lose focus by getting too caught up in the material things this world has to offer and neglect what's truly needed in one's life—and that's the Creator, our Heavenly Father.

So, we need to remember to put Him first and ask for His guidance in moments of needed clarity so that we will not go astray. I make sure to give Him thanks for everything that's going on in my life in good times or bad. Learn to be grateful for what you have, and don't focus on what you don't have.

He will give you peace to endure any situation, along with helping with your needs. There is always a way through; when God is in the picture, you must believe He is truly the only one and can do anything.

So, remember, whatever you want to accomplish can be done when you put Him at the front. He will help with the rest.

As you travel through this life of uncertainty, you can be sure that God will be there to help every step of the way.

Let the light of your Creator shine through to the man you want to be and are capable of being and allow Him to penetrate to the core of your spirit and illuminate the qualities that he has placed in you since birth. They have always been there although they may not have been used in a while; just waiting to be released and put to good use in your daily life. This can be you, like a true warrior for God seeking to do what's right in all situations. The power resides in you. You just need a spark of hope to ignite the flame that burns deep within you and drives you. So, you can do the right thing for yourself and your fellow man.

CHAPTER 2

BECOME ONE WITH ALL THINGS

Balance: an even distribution of weight enabling someone or something to remain upright and steady.

For a moment, imagine yourself as a child, playing on the seesaw at your local park. In order for this device to function properly, there needs to be an equal or close enough weight ratio on each side. This will allow the balance that is required to maintain the proper weight on both sides. This balancing act—without the proper weight—won't work. So, consider this when trying to balance your own life.

There are many parts to your life that must be taken care of, giving each part the attention it deserves. The three components—that are most vital—that should be carefully equaled out are your time, energy, and your responsibilities. These are key essentials in your daily routine. Developing structure keeps each one from overtaking the other; it takes a lot of self-discipline. Time is a luxury most of us don't have enough of, and it's one of the most valuable things we have. The way you dispense of it makes all the difference in how or what your day becomes.

There are 24 hours in our day, so at first glance, that seems like enough time to do as we please, but with another look at all the events that take up that 24-hour window, we quickly realize that time is fleeting. There is a time and place for everything we do. So, during that time, it's good to have your day thought out and planned. We need to make sure to set time aside for the really important things in life and set priorities. We all have different schedules and responsibilities, but you do have time. What you initially do with the time you have will ultimately determine what you become. First thing, you need to calculate how much time you have for work, self, friends, and family. You can start to divide your day accordingly. Work is your livelihood, so there will be little adjusting on that matter until you strike the right balance. Just don't work yourself into an early grave. Because we all need money to survive and enjoy life's many pleasures. But you don't need to spend all of your time in a day trying to acquire it. There has to be time for other things than just money. If you don't take care of yourself as a whole, you will never get to enjoy the money you do have. So, make sure to set time aside for the essentials in your life.

Try to keep work in its proper place. This will keep you from burning yourself out, and in turn, not being useful for anything else.

Realizing you're working too much is the first sign, then taking corrective measures would be the next step. Allowing time for yourself and your family is important, and taking care of your well-being is also key. You need sufficient allotted time to take good care of yourself. Making sure you have time for your needs is key for your well-being.

You need to make the most of your valuable time. Creating routines for yourself with the schedule you have can be really beneficial for the way you spend the time you have.

Try finding productive activities that are stimulating and beneficial. For example, things that you could do with a few hours of your time could be going for an evening walk, playing chess, or grounding. Grounding is sitting outside on the ground or walking outside barefoot in the grass. The earth has many health benefits when we connect to it. We should connect to it often.

Try to make the best use of your time—using it in the best ways possible. Watching TV for a bit is not bad, just don't let it consume all your time. You should always be attentive to the things or activities that are using up your time. If you do happen to watch more television than you would prefer, try to schedule programs that are informational or educational. There can be benefits to watching some TV programs when you are educating yourself. Try to keep from tuning into shows that only pertain to sex, violence, and drugs. This will ultimately start to pollute the brain as you fill it with nothing but this type of filth. Some of these shows may seem harmless at first, but the image and message it portrays can be damaging to the spirit and your overall being. So, just be mindful of the things that you allow in your mind and body. What you take in can make all the difference in how you feel and act.

Your energy and how it's dispensed throughout the day can determine what gets done and what doesn't get done. Energy is everywhere, but your energy is yours, so don't allow it to be drained all at once by the wrong things. You have a limited amount of energy, and when it's low or completely gone, you're no good to yourself or anyone else. So, remember to keep an eye on your energy and how much of it is being used in certain situations. You should look at it similar to a fuel gauge on your vehicle. When it has a full tank, you're ready to go and could ride all day. But when the gauge is on empty, you know if you don't stop and refuel soon, you'll be stuck on the side of the road. So, by maintaining awareness of your energy level, you will be able to balance out the amount you have and be able to distribute it efficiently.

There are people who love to drain your energy. Some do it intentionally while others do it unknowingly. Whichever the case, when this happens, make sure not to become a victim of it. Even if you have to be straight forward and remove yourself from the situation, then do that so you can refuel and get yourself together. Helping people is quite fine, but realizing that you can't help everyone is alright too, especially at the expense of destroying yourself—that's not alright. You have to be on constant alert to not drain your energy because you could be feeling fine one minute, then the next, you could feel completely drained and not even understand why.

For instance, you might be reading a book, then someone comes along to chat about a certain issue they may be having, and you listen, then give a reasonable response to their dilemma. After that, they leave, and you don't quite feel at ease like you did before. Your energy has just been drained, and that is the reason for the difference. Your energy is limited for one day, so you need to treat it as a limited resource not unlimited. By listening and engaging in their problems, it can zap your energy. You just have to be mindful of where it's going and how it's being used up and then pace yourself.

And the amount of energy you have each day will not be the same; some days you may feel like you're superman, and you can take on anything coming your way, and on other days, you may not know how you're even going to get through the day. That's just the way it goes sometimes, and it could be several reasons why you have a lack of energy. You may not be getting enough sleep at night—your environment and your health. Maintaining and keeping a healthy routine can be really helpful for maintaining and keeping a healthy balance of your energy. A couple of things I do every morning before the day gets started is take vitamins, drink water and a hot cup of tea. These simple things help get my day started on a good note. Small things can go a long way for one's energy.

Spread positive energy wherever you can. This can be really simple, just being kind and positive within yourself can help you do just that. There are always people watching you; you may not notice, but they are paying attention to the things you are doing and the things you are saying, so be mindful of this. It may seem that negative energy is almost everywhere—even taken over our entire planet—but it will be known that your energy is positive; you choose to be that way, and it will prevail. That's why it's so important to spread this message wherever you go, even if you never speak a word, it will become obvious. Positive energy is so much stronger than negative; that's why it doesn't stand a chance.

Do the things you need to do to stay positive, learn from the insight you have gained, and put it into practice in your life; the information will sustain you.

You may have many responsibilities in your life, but your primary responsibility is you, because if you're not alright then, how is anything else going to be taken care of? By making sure you're good, and that you're running on all cylinders, you will be able to reach your goals and handle your affairs. Friends and family are most likely a big part of the equation; your family comes first then your friends. They can really be a big factor in how your responsibilities are measured.

Make sure your friends and family know how you feel about them by the way you treat them. They are a part of the big picture and a valued part of your life. Be sure to hold them to the same high standards by being responsible as a true friend and part of your family. They play a major role in your life and deserve your time and energy. You just have to measure the amount of time that you give. Be intentional and give accordingly.

The family you are given is the only one you have, so appreciate them and always give your mother and father the respect they deserve. And appreciate your brothers and sisters and show them you love, and cherish the relationship you have with them. I do understand that the family you have means everything. But even with that, you still have an obligation to yourself. Sometimes, family members can be really taxing on you and even stress you out, draining all your time and energy. You are only one person and have needs and wants of your own. So, don't let others dictate your decisions when you clearly have set plans and goals.

You are human, and you have limited time and resources to give to people in your life. Form healthy habits that will help sort responsibilities out. Family can be some of the most draining of your time and energy if you are not careful. The manipulation tactic can also come into play and be quite successful at times. Don't allow people, even some family members to walk all over you, and drag you down. If you have people in your family that are not good for you, then it's perfectly alright to distance yourself from them. You can still communicate with them, but understand what it is they bring to the table. Don't allow them to be the cancer in your life—infecting you at every limb—cut them off and regain control. I understand that this is family, but you need to know that if you don't contain the situation with your family—especially if there is negativity involved, there may be a need to distance yourself. This is sadly the case that most people are all too familiar with. It's time to break the cycle; let's be better for our family and set a positive example for them to follow. So, in turn, you can be the one they look up to in leading them to a better course in life.

Having balance in the many aspects of your life will create a more even distribution of your responsibilities and how much time and energy you give to each one. This will help to give you a more successful way of taking care of your responsibilities. Not being overwhelmed by any one of them, but taking care of all of them. Having this understanding of balance and the way you should sort out your responsibilities can allow you to maintain a more resourceful method with the time and energy you have.

Taking care of each one of your responsibilities, individually and adequately, will allow you to maintain each of them successfully. Your life in turn becomes simpler and this creates peace of mind.

The way you balance your life now will lead you into more productive roles in the future. So, by giving each responsibility a certain amount of time and energy, you will create a better life for yourself.

By becoming one with all things in your life in a positive way, you will be setting yourself up for success and helping your family too. Having a healthy balance in your life will in turn allow room for other things—more opportunities in the future.

The power to accomplish these very things lies within you. You have the strength to achieve the very thing you set out to do.

Remember to keep the balance in check to make sure you're not being weighed down or pulled too much in either direction. By adjusting the scale, you will be able to view things more clearly. So, get started on balancing your day in a healthy and productive way, you will feel good about your life and in turn be a delight to be around.

A life that is balanced is a life that can be admired and enjoyed.

CHAPTER 3

HARNESS YOUR INNER VOICE

Focus: to produce a clear image.

Some of the most intriguing features of the human anatomy are the eyes. The ability to enhance the clarity of an image you see with a quick change of focus in the eye is nothing short of amazing. Having a clear focus on objects is truly a gift, now being able to focus on a particular task takes a whole new skill.

Your mind's eye can be the true focus on things you see and don't see but discern how they appear to you. Being able to look into each situation with true focus will enable you to see what's truly there from an insightful view.

When you take time to truly focus on what it is you're looking at, you can really see more than what meets the physical eye. Discernment about the things you see and visualize will increase your ability to focus intensely. Developing your own inner focus takes lots of work and practice. Being able to identify and listen to your inner voice involves more than your literal eye; you have to look below the surface. You have to block out all distractions to attach to this voice. You have the ability to do this; you just need stillness and clarity. Allow yourself to engage this focus so that you can block out any distractions you may encounter. Distractions are heavily integrated into everything we do; so being able to attain inner clarity is quite remarkable. But you need to acquire this trait in order to conquer these challenges insightfully. Let's say you're in traffic, and it's about 5:00 pm—rush hour, and everything is gridlock—and you're not moving but five feet every 5 minutes. This is enough to drive anyone up the wall and cause stress. That's when you turn your attention and focus to something positive, blocking out the annoying traffic jam and away from the current situation. You turn the radio on and vibe out to one of your favorite ballets, mellowing out in the meantime. Even turning the radio off and thinking about some good times you've had are helpful. Being able to make light of the situation and change your focus even adding some humor can be another way to shift your focus. The best thing about this is that it works most of the time.

Daydreaming can also be helpful, allowing your mind to wonder and then bringing it back into focus can be a good practice. Learning to turn your focus on and off on a particular issue is one way to harness your inner voice successfully.

We all have heard of how mirages can appear in your mind in the desert under extreme circumstances. The images that sometimes appear are not what they seem to be at first glance. This could be because we are in severe distress. Being able to focus under this amount of pressure will allow you to maintain clarity even in the most dramatic situations you face. So, when the image of what you're seeing comes into focus, make sure you're seeing things clearly and with insight. Like a mirage, some things are not what they appear to be, so don't be too quick to judge or conclude you have all the facts until you have a greater understanding of what it is you are looking at. This in turn will allow you not to give merit to things and situations that appear one way but may be another.

Your inner voice will allow you to view situations with discernment. Extreme focus can allow you to achieve the most remarkable goals because you are so focused and not distracted. It will enable you to endure any ordeal with peace and concentration. No matter how hectic things sometimes get, this type of focus will help the outcome be a successful one. You might have projects that you are working on, that may be hard to finish or to even get started on. The amount of undivided attention and focus you give to each project will determine the outcome. Having clarity and focus on the project internally and then outwardly is key, giving it your full attention. You will be giving merit to the inner quality and not just the outward appearance, producing better results.

Learn to visualize; even if you see an image clearly, look beyond the obvious. This can provide accurate details about the image's inner quality. So, when you come in contact with any image or situation, engage your focus so that you are able to distinctively interpret the situation correctly. There are several displays of focus you should be aware of. There is out of focus—not being able to quite see the image at all. Then there is blurred focus where you can see a slight view of the image but can't quite make it out. Lastly, there is in focus—in complete focus where the image is clear and you can clearly make out what you're looking at. While you're trying to improve your inner focus, learn from the animals in nature. They really have great focus, especially when it comes to capturing prey. One that comes to mind is the cheetah trying to catch the gazelle. The amount of extreme focus it must require while it's trying to catch its meal. Waiting in the trenches while the gazelle graze nearby the cheetah's territory. The thing is the cheetah has a limited fuel tank before it goes on low fuel. It is able to run at high rates of speed like 60 to 70 mph for just about a minute or so. So, its timing has to be accurate when choosing the exact time to launch after its prey for the attack. All of this comes down to the amount of focus the cheetah applies to the task at hand, and with any distractions, he would not stand a chance. Because if the timing isn't just right, the cheetah will run out of energy, and the gazelle will live for another day, leaving the feline to seek out another opportunity later on. The lesson here for us is "You can only really focus on one thing at a time."

Another fascinating creature to admire is the hawk. This amazing bird is one of the most agile birds of prey we know of. This bird's sight alone is something like binoculars when compared to humans; the prey of their liking is the field mouse and other smaller birds. The amount of focus this bird has is amazing. This bird can see a mouse in the field from about a mile in the sky—very impressive. Yeah, this is about how high it is when it sees its soon-to-be meal in the fields and comes in for the kill.

The amazing focus this bird must have to achieve his goal from such a high altitude. We can learn from animals and how they are so focused. They are precise and deliberate, keeping their goal in sight. Any distraction or slightest mistake can cause this bird to not have dinner for the evening. These are some examples you can look at when trying to evaluate the level of focus that goes into certain events. So, you can apply this same amount of determination when trying to achieve a certain task. The ability to focus under extreme situations will be the most challenging. But the end result will be the most rewarding; learn to be at one with your inner voice. It will save you in times you need it most because sometimes, the outer surface of situations can look alright to the physical eye, but with the mental eye, you can see things that only a trained individual will be able to see and save yourself from potentially drawing the wrong conclusion about any situation.

Harnessing your concentration and focusing to be at one with your inner voice will allow you to have more depth and meaning in life. While you're focusing on a particular image or situation, try to see beneath the surface. There are many layers to an individual. When people try to hide some things from you and others, they may want you to notice. Focus on the body language of people and be discerning, then your inner voice will guide you. It will secretly alert you about what's going on with this person. Some of the things they will be doing will be a red flag, telling you to run for the hills as fast as you can. Other signals will be telling you to help them just not broadcasting it loudly. Maybe helping them privately, with a matter they have. Look to be helpful when finding yourself encountering these types of situations. You could be really helping someone improve their lives and not even realizing it at the time.

So, try to focus and see these things when dealing with people; you could really be providing help for someone going through a tough time. Having a certain depth to your focus will lead you to be more in tune when dealing with certain situations. When you're able to truly focus on your inner voice and how far your depth can go, you will become focused on an entirely new level, especially when you see with a deeper understanding. This will enable you to see the situation from a bird's eye view, so to speak. It can really be useful in all that you do in life. This clarity will come when you look deeper than what's on the surface. Most issues are not on the surface, So by being able to dig deeper, you will uncover all the different layers of a person and maybe promote much needed healing in the process.

There are so many hurting souls in the world, it's upsetting to even think about. Our help can be there to soothe and comfort them when they need it the most. A simple glance in their direction with a smile can heal simple wounds, but stopping to ask if someone is okay when it looks like they may need a shoulder to lean on can break the ice, create the opportunity to offer an encouraging word, and change their outlook on life.

You can be the lamp that lights their darkness in their most desperate time of need. Let's be helpful with this renewed focus you have. There is a lot of good to be done with it if used properly. You want to always stay focused on the task at hand giving it your full attention. The time you put into someone can say a lot about the person you are. But the amount of focus and attention you give an individual in need can create a lasting relationship for life. You will be so surprised at the way people respond to the way you focus on them for just a few minutes.

For the moment, it might not seem like such a big deal, but to them it is a big deal. This might be just what they needed at that time. And there's no price you can put on that. By being able to do this, you will be helping out in such a monumental way but not even realize it. In today's world, there is a lack of focus on the important things in life. There seems to be more apathy than anything else. Let's change the cycle and give people some glimmer of hope when they encounter us, so they will feel like there's a positive change in the world that they are living in. Maybe by the grace of our God, it will help them see another day and start to develop a more caring attitude for themselves and the world they live in. This way of living is so rewarding in its own way. Being able to focus on the needs of others is such a selfless service; it deserves commendation. When you develop this keen sense of focus, you will be able to tackle personal matters with greater success and help others to do the same. Also, allowing you to see into issues or situations clearer and maybe be of assistance to others when you can. So, let's keep a clear focus, listen to that inner voice, and improve those skills as you put them to good use. And in the end, receive the renewed focus you've always had in sight.

CHAPTER 4

HOW TO BE ON STANDBY

Patience: the capacity to accept or tolerate delay, trouble, or suffering without getting angry or upset.

Notice the process of how a diamond is made; it's quite astounding how this amazing work of art is transformed into a beautiful gem. In order for this rare beauty to reach its full potential, patience is necessary, all while undergoing extreme amounts of constant pressure that allow the shape to take form.

There is no mistake in the procedure it must undergo to obtain the purest quality possible. Can you think of anything of true quality that doesn't require a waiting period as part of the process?

Our world is full of creations that were developed over long periods of time. Some things that come to mind are dams, bridges, and locomotives. Without the patient development required during the process to complete such structures, they would not be able to stabilize our world without a catastrophic impact.

Look at how long it takes to create another human being. The 9-month period it takes to create a baby is quite amazing, but it's a process and requires patience for everything to develop properly. Even as a person develops, time is needed. Especially for the male brain, it doesn't fully develop until 25 years of age.

Let's say you want to be an elite tennis player, and this truly is your dream. You're not going to wake up one morning and be the great tennis player you want to be without putting in the work. It takes work and patience to become this great tennis player that has the talent to acquire what it takes to achieve top-level performance.

Everything about this process takes patience. Your skill level will take time to reach its full potential. The opportunity to really showcase your talent may not happen or be there when you want it to be; it may take longer than you would like, and this is all part of the program. But by not being impatient, you can and will achieve the very goal you set out to reach.

You should get really familiar with being patient because as long as you're striving for better, this will be part of the equation. The sooner you grasp the idea and come to terms with it being part of your life, the easier it will be to experience it when it comes along and requires you to be just that—patient. And it won't be such a shock to the system and be so uncomfortable in the process. I'm sure we've all heard the saying "Patience is a virtue." Well, this is very true and quite necessary for the success of your future. I do realize that no one really enjoys waiting for things to happen. But this can also be a good thing if you look at it from another perspective.

Acquiring patience will be beneficial in many ways. For example, when a new hot item hits the shelf, instead of rushing out to get this new item, wait a bit until the price drops or to see the reviews it gets after some consumers have tested it out.

This will save you time and money down the line. Let the ones who always have to be first at everything enjoy this product and let them test it out for you.

Sometimes in life, the first becomes last, and the last becomes first. And what I mean by that is that the ones who are always the first to receive are put last, and the same goes for the ones that are always last to receive they will become first for a change. Things have a way of balancing out. The ones that are always first in line could receive defective items, and the ones that are last could receive a more secure item. Sometimes, things just work out this way. It's not always beneficial to be first to receive. One reason would be that it would begin to make you feel like you're an entitled individual, feeling like you should be first, have it now, and never have to wait. This would not be productive for you and your overall growth.

Learning that the world doesn't always revolve around you and that you're not the only person on the planet will continually keep you in check and down to earth. Learning how to be on standby will help to develop the skills to become a more patient person.

Think about all the food that is available to you. Now, visualize the fast food that you can have at a moment's notice that will not leave you satisfied most of the time. Then you have a healthy meal that takes time to prepare, these meals leave you feeling full and satisfied, along with providing the nutrition your body needs to function properly.

By learning to appreciate being patient, it will, in turn, allow you to gain insight into the maturity process that will be a direct result of being patient. Going through this process will help you achieve this quality in its truest form and will serve as an asset to your development. It will give you the ability to observe things in their premature stage and when it has truly reached maturity. This will help you when looking into certain situations and learning how to be patient as they develop. This can also be an enjoyable, enlightening experience as well. Watching people grow in their efforts to be better and to mature and helping them to also be patient by your own example will have a positive influence on them. We have to constantly be patient with the people we love and care about. Everyone doesn't bloom at the same time, so let's give them the time too. Taking time to be patient with them will help the relationship prosper. You just have to see the beauty in the process when it might be difficult to do so.

The many transformations that are a necessary part of life and we must go through can be a truly delightful experience if we embrace them. Remember when we were young kids living like there was no tomorrow, we didn't have a care in the world, but the one thing we couldn't wait for was to get older. Knowing what we know now, most of us would have liked to stay that young for a little while longer. We couldn't wait to be older than we were, so we could do what all the grownups were doing. We were all in such a rush to become adults. And we were all in for a rude awakening once we reached adulthood.

Not taking time to appreciate the age we were at. For most of us, it was some of the best years of our lives. Especially in hindsight, realizing how good we had it with little to no responsibilities, most of us wish we could go back to those very moments in time, especially looking at the way the world is right now.

Well, those days are over, but the good thing is we have grown up and we have come into the person we are now. We can still have good memorable times in this day in age. We just have to be more thoughtful about the things we do because every decision we make has long-lasting effects on us. So, we need to be careful with all our choices—be patient and make good choices.

Learning to appreciate life at every stage is the goal—life is beautiful at every stage—in its own particular way. Being patient at all of these stages is really key. Certain stages in life bring tools into your life that you can use to correct some of the issues you might have had in the past. These tools will be there for you in your mental tool kit, so you can use them throughout your life whenever you run into a dilemma that you may not know how to correct in the beginning. We don't always have the answers when we want them. By being patient, we can learn to wait on them, and in due time, they will be revealed to us. In some cases, we might not be ready for the so-called answers we want, at the time we want them. Then they might be delivered at a more appropriate time when we can handle them better. Timing is truly everything; it's not always on the time we want, but it can be and most likely will be at the time when we need it most, and that can really make all the difference.

Learning to expect good things to come from being patient will allow you a measure of comfort during the process. You will see being patient as a part of growing up and becoming the person you would like to be. Look for ways to increase your patience. This will add to your arsenal in your tool kit and prepare you for moments when you really need to depend on being patient to get you through to the other side without coming undone. There are really not a lot of situations that don't require you to exercise a measure of patience.

By applying this quality every chance you get, you become a work-in-progress, and you will already be prepared for the task before it gets to you. You always have to stay ready, so you don't have to get ready when it comes. By adopting this practice, it will allow you to rise above situations that may test your patience. You might even surprise yourself with "Wow! I really waited in line for almost an hour just to get gas and didn't lose my cool in the process." This is an achievement. Believe me! The way that you handle simple events leads you to progress in more serious matters.

The way road rage incidents are constantly erupting is ridiculous, to say the least. Just because someone wanted the parking spot you were in or you cut them off in traffic by mistake. We now live in a world where people don't want to wait for anything, and if they don't get it that instant, everything can escalate until it's out of control. They now want to take matters to the furthest extent. Now, they want to lash out at you, or someone else—sometimes the person these people lash out at—had nothing to do with the initial problem. So that's why I say being patient can save your life and also someone else's that might not know that their life is even in any danger at the time. This problem we're seeing is due to having everything at our fingertips whenever we want it. Our society has created this problem, and we've become so out of touch with reality. They think this is how we're supposed to be. Having access to things whenever we want them and never having to wait for anything. Well, that's not normal, and it's an unhealthy way to think. That's not the real world; it's not real life. So be part of the solution and not part of the problem, and we'll make out just fine.

Every action has a reaction, so the action you take can determine a lot. So be mindful of everything you do. There is a domino effect to everyone's actions. In some form or fashion, they affect those around us regardless if they had anything to do with the event or not. Just being near can be enough to have an impact on others. So, by acquiring this trait, you can really save yourself a lot of difficult times in the future. Waiting patiently for something isn't going to ruin your day; it just might save the day.

You wouldn't believe how some of these simple decisions we make cause such a ripple effect in our life. So, if you're ever in a situation where you find yourself with an impatient person and they are in such a hurry and they insist on going before you, let them go. Whether you're standing in line or driving in traffic, just move aside and let them go ahead of you. In our world today, common sense isn't too common, so you will need to think for others by remaining patient with them. By doing this, you will be removing yourself from a situation that isn't stable and could escalate out of control. This in turn could really be saving you or the other person involved, and potentially, the people that might be around you from any danger that may have come from any unstable person you may come in contact with. So, put being patient at the top of your list of things you need to do, and it will put you in the safe zone, avoiding people's reckless behavior and helping you overcome many situations you may encounter.

CHAPTER 5

EMBRACE THE SILENCE

Peace: freedom from quarrels and disagreements; harmony.

While the sun is starting to peak over the horizon, and your day is about to begin. Briefly give thought to you having a peaceful day and allowing peaceful thoughts to reside within you. You doing this will allow you to start your day off on a positive note.

The thoughts you decide to concentrate on will usually carry over and can affect the outcome of your day. What you think will become who you are. The thoughts you decide to keep around are what you will become, so be cautious of your thoughts.

Having peace of mind is everyone's desire for the most part. In a chaotic world, we all seek peace where there is madness. But sometimes, the peace we yearn for isn't in sight. That's when we need to look inside ourselves and search for solace deep within our being.

You'll have to shut out the world and concentrate on the peace and cut ties with all distractions at the moment to obtain this peace. Find a favorite memory of yours and go there whenever you're searching for solace. The environment you're in might not allow the peace you're looking for, so then you must go to your happy place within to escape the noise because let's be honest, we all can't wear noise cancellation headphones all day long to avoid the racket. So, that's why we have to have an escape route that's not too far away.

This will allow you to remain at peace through any ordeal, not losing sight of yourself. Realizing that nothing stays the same, and every situation changes in due time will help with your current situation if it's not as peaceful as you would like. Letting you know that your situation will change in one way or another for the better, just give it a chance.

The amount of noise that's placed in our brain daily is quite the overload, to say the least. From the people in our immediate circle to the traffic sirens throughout the town. It's ingrained in every aspect of our lives. So, at the first chance you get, turn the noise off. If you can, separate yourself from everyone momentarily and mute all the noise. So, you can at least collect your own thoughts for a moment to help relieve some of the tension you may be feeling. Doing this will allow you to clear your head and find peace within yourself. Silence can be a great thing, even a healing method for the mind. When all the sounds of information have ceased for a while, we actually feel like we can go on with the remainder of our day.

The constant amounts of information overloading our brain receptors daily are not productive for our peace of mind. Certain types of information can distort our peace by the negative concepts they give off, so be selective on what you let in.

All of us deserve peace, but all of us don't have peace or live in places where there is peace. A lot of places around the world are not at peace and are at war at this very moment and long for peace desperately. So, while we might be in places where peace is absent around us, we can still be at peace within our very selves.

Embracing the silence will allow you to reach the peace that you most desire to carry you through your day with little or no complaints. The silence is a major part of you being at peace. Learning how to keep silent during stressful times will allow you to not act out while you might not be feeling your absolute best. When people cause issues with you, try your best to be peaceful with them. They may be looking for a reason to act out on you. Don't give them one, even if they're in the wrong, remain peaceful during the entire interaction. They will be expecting you to respond negatively. Not responding harshly to the attitude they may be giving you will in turn change the attitude of the individual you're encountering and may allow them to have a change of heart in the way they might have acted toward you. Having them look at their own actions in an undesirable light. Always being the bigger person in negative situations, you will be putting water on the fire, so you can extinguish the flames. Instead of adding fuel to the fire and igniting the situation, both parties go up in smoke and ruin their lives. So always take the high road even when it's hard and not your fault. Always keeping the peace in most situations will almost certainly give you a good outcome. You will be thankful eventually and rewarded by avoiding situations that can lead to harmful outcomes in the present and the future. When people are not peaceful, still respond with kindness and peace. In other words, as far as it depends on you, be at peace with all people.

This will show people that they don't get to you and that you have control over the peace that resides deep within. Hopefully, in some manner, this will allow them to see the error of their ways, and maybe reconsider their actions in the future. When you show people this way of living it will give them a sense of satisfaction in their life. Letting them know that they don't have to be negative and miserable their whole life. They too can find peace as well; they just have to let go of the anger that's holding them down like an anchor. Then they can receive the peace; they've been searching for. Not realizing that it was in them the entire time and waiting for them to finally seek it, so it could be found. Once we realize that peace isn't bought, it's given, then we can start to understand a little more about what it takes to obtain this peace.

Our God and the creator of all things good, holy, and true is the only one who can give us the peace that surpasses all understanding. No one else has this ability. There is a false sense of peace that comes from drugs, but once they wear off, you're back to square one, feeling empty and still seeking solace. The peace God provides never wears off; it's everlasting, give it a try you'll see and include him in your life. So, if you have been striving for peace in your life and haven't been able to have any success in the matter, God is the answer, and there's no way around that; he will give you the peace you never thought you could have. So, once you have the true understanding of where the source of our peace comes from, you can then truly start to tap into your true potential. We are all part of something much higher than ourselves and the success we have in life starts with acknowledging that fact. We are truly servants of God; we were put here to serve him and to do his will. Meanwhile, enjoy the many pleasures he provides for us daily.

Somewhere down the line, we may have gotten disconnected, but it's never too late to get the train back on the tracks so to speak. Once we know what the right thing is, we just have to do it, and it's as simple as that. Because we now know how to live justly—doing what's right—so there are no more excuses about it. When we decide to live according to our Heavenly Father, our lives become so much better and simpler. The stresses that we use to have are like water off a ducks back. We're at peace with the life we have and the time we have on earth. We learn to appreciate things on a deeper level. Deep, like the bottom of the ocean. We look for meaning and peace wherever we reside. You want to infect people with peace, spread it wherever you can.

I can't express how much we as people are in such desperate need of this peace at an alarming rate. So, be the peacemaker in your walks and travels throughout your day. You become at peace with yourself and others. What you become will allow you to remain at peace when situations arise that are not so peaceful. You will triumph over them with no problem, keeping your inner peace. So, whenever you need peace at your side, just remember it's on the inside where the peace resides, always ready to take you to a place of calm. With everything you do, there needs to be practice and effort taken to reach new heights. You can obtain the peace you need to endure the struggles of life. While we live in a society where they tell you to just go out and sort your problems out with what amounts to a band-aid, throwing money at it or reacting in anger is only a temporary fix and not a solid one. When we realize that life's issues can't all be mended by the currency we provide, the better we will be able to handle things more appropriately. Let's not cover the issue; let's cure it with the appropriate measures that need to be taken. Heal the problem at the source, so it doesn't recirculate and become an issue again. Otherwise, the cycle will just continue until you get totally engulfed by it.

Take time to create a safe space where you reside in peace or where you can isolate yourself from everyone around you. This will be for an hour or so a day where you can reflect on your day and be at peace with yourself and your thoughts. This will help you build a barrier of peace around you without anyone else being present that can disrupt the peace. You should be at peace being alone; you shouldn't need anyone around you to obtain peace. It's perfectly alright to spend time alone to get a full understanding of yourself. This will help you develop the peace you need to endure each day. If you always keep people around you, this will start to affect your inner peace. So, make sure to allow yourself the independent alone time to gather your thoughts and get yourself refueled.

It's easy to get caught up in being smothered by people and objects, not providing quality time for yourself each day. By dealing with only the needs of others, eventually, you will be taking on more than you're able to, which in turn breaks you down later on down the line because you failed to give yourself alone time. And not really understanding why at the time because you're so caught up in everyone and everything around you to really even notice that you need to step back and take care of yourself. Then you're forced to step back because you hit the bottom, and you may feel like you can't endure another moment. This can happen and when it does, it's time to step back and turn it around. We don't have to over-exert ourselves down to the bone to be appreciated by the people around us. It's alright to take time out of your day to provide a little self-care. If they're truly in your corner, they will understand, and it won't cause any strife. Remember, the people in your life matter, but you need to make sure of your priority because it's your life, and you only get one go around, so take care of yourself.

The peace you allow yourself will come with discipline, so be adamant about keeping it protected. Learning how to tune things out for a moment of peace may be a constant challenge but worth the effort. You can achieve peace even with all the chaos in the world. But it will take lots of practice. It seems like there is always something trying to disturb the peace you have. That's why you have to be on constant watch for peace invaders that come within your border.

The peace you provide for yourself will allow you to be at ease with any situation you encounter. This peace will keep you calm in times when the average person would be losing their temper. Remaining at peace with others will give you profound insight. People will wonder how it is that you are able to remain at such peace despite a stressful situation.

Being at peace with whatever you're going through will make you a more appreciative person. Once you learn to incorporate it, you will find that it's an effective way to enjoy a better, calmer life. Anything worth having is going to take time to develop. So, allow time to learn this skill and make it a daily practice. These techniques for being at peace will serve you well and create peace within.

Your peace is the ultimate solution to surviving situations without coming untethered in the process. So, practice being at peace whenever you can as this will help in every situation, and you will see the benefits when applied. You will learn to see things in a whole new light, giving you a new look at life.

CHAPTER 6

HAVE OPEN ARMS

Love: deep affection and warm feelings for another.

There is one form of expression that truly has a universal appeal to every individual. This expression that I'm speaking of is one that has the ability to heal one's heart. Indeed, love is the only expression that has the power to really communicate with a broken heart.

Everyone can mostly agree that the effect love has on people can really determine the outcome of many things. Most of us love and have love for the things we care about or that we hold close to our hearts.

Can you for a moment imagine what the world would be like if there was no love in it? Well, at this point, it may seem like the world is without the presence of love, looking at the way things are starting to unfold. The hate in our world is severe and getting stronger as the world turns. No one wants to live in a world that's filled with hate, with absence of love.

The only way to truly combat hate is through the power of love. Love is so strong; it can overpower hate. It will prevail no matter what the battle and throughout eons of time. Being able to have love for yourself is so crucial to being able to display any form of affection towards anyone else. Because how do you plan on showing others love, when you don't even love yourself? So, make sure to love yourself fully first before you try to love anyone else. Your understanding of what love is and what it looks like will allow you to identify it when you come in contact with it. In turn, allowing you to reciprocate when it's shown to you. This will show that you have a true appreciation for it and don't take it for granted. The word "love" is verbally expressed so carelessly in many instances in life. People will say it to one another, without really having any meaning behind it. The meaning of it doesn't go along with the action of the one saying it. This word should only be used in the form of having a deep affection for someone or something. This word is too commonly used today; it's used without the action that should follow—an outward display of the feelings within. Do not say this word unless your intent is true, and you really mean it; this should remain a sacred word to you. When you are expressing love to someone, make sure they understand the depth of how you truly feel about them. No matter how much you tell someone you love them, it isn't going to matter unless there are actions behind the words. The only way to know that a person loves you is by the actions it prompts. Let no one tell you anything different; love requires expression.

People on the receiving end actually want to believe the things that people they care about are saying to them because they do love and care about them. So, when these individuals are telling you the things you want to hear, make sure they line them up with their actions, to see if what they're saying is really accurate and true. Sometimes, people hurt the very people that they confess to love the most.

This is an all too common cycle that needs to be broken because it's not really fair for the people that would go above and beyond for the ones they love. Ways to avoid doing this is by putting yourself in the other person's shoes to really get an understanding of how hurtful it really is when you fail to live up to the promises made. Another way is by trying to visualize yourself living without these special people you have in your life. Because that's going to be the result if you don't man up and do right by the people who always have your back. These are the people that are your backbone because they will be there to hold you up when you're not strong enough to do it on your own.

So, you really don't know how hard it can really be on your own when you're left in the dark because they are fed up with the constant garbage you keep giving them. So, let's not let it get to that point; you can turn it around and show them that you actually have love for them. The thing is, don't say things you don't mean, and that you're not going to live up to in the end. Keep things simple and don't make commitments you can't handle. This will keep you from coming up short in your attempts because you can't do the things you told them you could. Everyone wants to be loved along with being givers of love. Being true to the person you are and the people around you will help you become a true person of love. Many people have loved others and been hurt as a result, so they might find it difficult to love others. Don't be hard on these people, and allow them time to adjust and get through the heartbreak. They may be able to love again if they see that the love you have to give is pure and true. Don't cause them to reconsider, due to your actions not reflecting the words you're expressing. Telling people the truth is really all they want; it's really how you present yourself in an honest way. Display yourself in a way where people can feel like they can trust you and can tell you anything without you judging them. They will see you as a person with a loving heart, loving all people, and willing to help people when you can. Because we are all people who have basic needs, let's be the person we want to be known as, a loving person. Love is the strongest emotion known on the entire planet.

One of the strongest forms of love I have experienced is a mother's love, especially the unconditional love she has for her children. It is truly beautiful. Moments of love on display. It's honestly some of the most precious love I have witnessed, with my own mother. I'm sure a lot of people can agree with me on the subject. There's almost nothing you can do to escape the love of a mother that really cares for her children. The amount of love and affection I've experienced from my mother has really formed the individual I am today. Learning to love deep within my own heart. I try to pass this love along as I engage with other people letting them know that they too can be loved. Even if you didn't receive a similar love or upbringing as a young person, you too can receive love like that of a mother and strong feelings of affection from others in your own life when you live a life based on love. This love I'm referring to is called "Agape." The love of God—God's love; the true creator of love. God is love, and we are His children, so He will give His ultimate love to us. We are created in His image, so the qualities He has, reside deep within us as well. All you have to do is seek His love, and you will be a receiver of it, then imitate him in your own life.

A mother's love is quite special, but it doesn't compare to the love God has in store for you. The reason is that He knows what you truly need even if you're not totally sure. Even if you as a child didn't receive the motherly love children deserve, God can give you this love plus much more; you just have to walk in the light. He will clothe you with warmth and the purest of love and affection you have ever encountered in your existence.

I stand behind these words I share with you. He is living, and He is true; He will mend you and give you more love than you ever imagined was possible. Just seek Him first. That's all He asks of you. This is not requiring too much from you. The reason He wants you to do His will is that He loves you, and He knows what is best for you. Even if you think you do, He knows better. He just wants you to live up to the potential He sees in you. He is truly your biggest fan, and whether you agree with him or not, He's in your corner rooting for you and your success.

The ultimate reward is being in God's favor and living by His guidance. So if you're looking for love—pure love—by being shown the proper way to express love, God will help you develop the expression of love that everyone is desperately searching for. There is no other way to experience this level of love in any other form other than through God. So, when you love or truly learn how to love, exude it with every fiber of your being. You in turn will be reflectors of the love that has been shown to you, and you can spread this love wherever you go. So, don't allow hate to reside in your heart, we don't have enough time on this earth for hate, and it's so unnecessary. It really takes more energy expressing hate than it does love. People do often give us reasons to resent them and even diminish the love we have for them, but we can't live in the shadows of the past because it's not healthy for us, and it's not going to help us move forward in life. Give people a chance to change because none of us are perfect, and we all are trying to figure life out as we go.

By replacing the hate with the love you have, you will be helping people see that there are people in their life that truly love them. Sometimes, you have to show people the way—leading by example—before they really get the big picture. Be the person that gives love and shows others how to love even when it may be hard to do. Let's be honest, sometimes the people we have in our lives are really hard to love because of the actions they display. And some people are much worse than others, but even with that being true, we still have to look past their imperfections and display acts of love whenever we can. Let's be real; we all may have been a little hard to deal with at one time or another. So we need to be mindful of our own imperfections as well as others.

Remember if we don't forgive others when they trespass against us, our heavenly father is not going to forgive us either. So, we need to always remember to let bygones be bygones and move on, so you too can progress as well. So let's love as hard and pure as humanly possible, letting the light shine so brightly that it's almost blinding to others observing us. That is the way we should all be striving to live.

Have open arms, so that you can receive the love given to you, and send love out to others.

CHAPTER 7

TAKE TIME TO UNDERSTAND

Empathy: the ability to identify with or understand another's situation or feelings.

When you look at the world before you, you may notice that there is something quite significant missing, and has been for some time now. That would be empathy. As your path intersects with people, it seems like they only care about one thing, and this would be themselves—it's like they're obsessed with themselves. It's really quite disheartening the more you see such things. The more time that goes by, it appears to be getting worse at a rapid rate. People are not even trying to understand what's going on in another person's life.

It really has become the norm in our society today. Everywhere you turn you can see the lack of concern for others. This is truly why I believe our world is suffering the way it is.

If others could just take a moment out of their day to put someone first other than themselves, I believe we could resolve the miscommunication we encounter daily.

We are all different in many ways, and that's the beauty of the world we live in. We all contribute in some way to the many facets that make up our world, and that's the beauty of life.

People that are different from you have just as much of a right as you to pursue their goals, hopes, and dreams. They want a successful life, and desire to live in a safe environment as each of us hopes for.

Although we all may be different, we can still learn something from each other if we would take the time to understand the other person. Instead of just writing them off before we get a chance to know people, why not take a moment to really understand the reason why a person acts the way they do or what makes a person the way they are? It could be revealed to us as we listen, and the results may surprise us if we would just allow time to get to know a person.

I do believe it is causing people great harm by not giving them the time of day. Empathy is really the missing link in the world we live in. The things we could learn about others if we would just apply a little empathy and show concern for those around us.

People are suffering in such a way that it should be obvious and alarming to anyone that is paying attention. The world we once knew is slowly slipping away from us. It has changed. And it doesn't look like we're going to get it back. The damage has taken its toll.

Being able to identify and understand someone may take some time to develop. But it is possible. Just taking time to figure out why a person is the way they are, does not really require as much effort as you think. You just have to be willing to set yourself aside, look at others, and seek to be of help to them. Because the effort you put forth to understand the person you are engaging with will require your full attention. So, if you put someone else's needs above your own; for a moment, you might actually be able to obtain empathy in your life. Just being able to listen to someone without cutting them off in the middle of speaking. Listening intently, gaining an understanding of who they are and what they are really about, and all that it entails, is what empathy is all about. To the average person, empathy may not seem like a big deal, but to people that really understand empathy—really know that it is a quality we need in this world—they put a high value on it. Having empathy will make you seem like a hero to some people because it may be just what they need.

Really, empathy can be compared to the water you drink. Let me explain: if your drinking water is not up to environmental protection agency standards, it will cause you to develop health issues if the quality of water is not changed. The same concept applies to the lack of empathy; if you don't show people this quality, don't try to feel what they are going through then it could have a negative effect on them. They might start out alright, but over time, they're going to feel like nobody understands them, and that no one wants to or ever will. Then they might turn to self-medicating to numb the pain, and once they figure out that this doesn't work, it gets worse from there. It can lead a person to spiral downward because we are seeing it at an alarming rate—resulting in suicides. Yes, it's very real in our world and growing every day because people don't know who to turn to or feel they don't have people that have any true understanding of them.

Empathy or the lack thereof, is very important in life. Today, we all need to cultivate it. And until we start taking it more seriously, then we're going to continue to see a world that lacks this vital quality.

And I know no one wants to see these tragic events take place, especially with the people we know, love, and care about. But that will be the result, and if we do not change our ways, it could be detrimental to our overall well-being.

Let's try something; let's put others before ourselves and give them an opportunity to tell us what's going on with them. I know sometimes we don't really want to do certain things because we're tired or whatever the reason may be. But this is of the utmost importance, a moment of our time could really be saving the people we pass by daily or the people we have in our own life.

I am sure you will be quite amazed at the things you may hear from them. We might even realize that even with us being different, there are some similarities that we may have in common that we couldn't have guessed in a million years by our first impression of them.

Think about it! We're all on this planet learning from the people we have around us.

Sometimes, we need a helping hand in dealing with our daily struggles. If you truly want to help your neighbor, look inside yourself and make some room for empathy. Being able to apply this in your life can really be saving someone else's in the process.

You just don't know what people are going through, and a lot of times, they don't feel comfortable enough to even tell anyone because they feel like no one even cares or they're concerned about what people may think of them.

You have to be the one that cares for the people around you; this should be your duty to uphold. Because if you don't do it, then who will? Just expressing that you're willing to take the time to understand someone you meet is enough to start the conversation. It may allow them to open up to you in ways they've never opened up to anyone else.

This could really be a breakthrough for them and for you. Giving someone else hope to see another day is what you could be doing. Most of the time, people are not going to tell us how close they may be to the edge, and this is typical in that state of mind.

But if we as people will feel for others, which is the opposite of the world around us, then we in turn can be the hand that pulls someone away from the cliff they may be close to falling off.

The thing is we might not have anything in common with some people, but that has nothing to do with showing them that they too can be cared for and that they still matter. We are all uniquely made to contribute in one way or another. When we are talking with people, allow them to share what they have to say without interrupting them. This will tell them that you are really listening and that you really care about the things they're telling you.

This in turn will allow them to express more deeply hidden issues they may have but don't necessarily want to share. You being able to gain someone's confidence is really a thing of beauty.

And you could do this the first time you meet someone by the actions you display. People everywhere are looking for someone to confide in and desperately want someone that can take the time to understand the person they are, along with the situation they may be going through.

You could really be changing the course of someone's life if you would just show a little understanding in your approach. You could really be changing that person's life for the better with the newfound ability you have to show more empathy.

The empathy you reflect will allow you to peel each layer of the person back until you reach the core of the issue, in turn identifying the problem and possibly mending it as well. If we could, for a moment, put ourselves in the other person's situation. It may give us some clarity about why the person is the way they are, along with why they're experiencing their current issues. Allowing us to fully understand them, and not judge them at all for it. Because people can't control the way they were raised as a child, and the things that might have happened to them during that stage in their life, this makes them the way they are now, due to no fault of their own.

Let people express to you what they feel and why they feel this way. The experiences we go through make us the people we initially become. People may have been put through the wringer, may have been living with a void in their life for a long time, or may just need a listening ear to turn things around.

You can be there to rescue them from the tidal wave that is about to crash over them which will drag them to the bottom of the ocean floor. So, let's be known as empathic people by those we encounter in our daily life. By developing this quality, you in turn will help others see the value and even encourage them to imitate you and change for the better. We all want people to understand us, even if it's just one person. Sometimes, that's all it takes—for just one person to make the changes in someone's life. They're not looking for a hundred people to take interest in them and understand them. They just need one individual that can understand what they're going through, to make all the difference in the world for them.

Once we come to terms with how we need to go back to the simple way of living, we will be so much better. We have to stop trying to live up to society's standards because once you fail to reach the standards of the world, you tend to feel empty inside like you're worthless. This is definitely not the case; you're not worthless, nor have you ever been. Try living up to a higher standard—God's standards. This always gets the best results—I'm sure of it. And if you mess up in the process, He won't ridicule you or discard you as a result. He will in fact help you more, help you reach your goals, and develop qualities that make your life better. He only wants the best for you as a parent would their child. The thing is that He will not force you to agree with Him. He will just show you that there's no other right way but His way. And He will let you choose your own path, experiencing what comes along with it. Hoping that in the end, you will see that the only true way is God's way. He made us and knows what kind of people he created us to be: kind, loving, and empathetic.

And that is the truth because God is the truth, and that's all He will ever be. That's something you can always count on. There's no way around that. You just have to believe, and He will prove it to you every time, without fail. He is just waiting for you to put him to the test, and the rest will be taken care of. He will bring out all the beauty he sees deep within you; that you may have lost sight of.

Allow him to take over your life, you won't regret it.

Living this way is going to give you a better life and good results. The empathy you acquire will have a huge impact on your life and the people you decide to share it with.

So, take time to understand everyone you encounter. You never know what can come of it. You just might learn something that you can relate to, in turn learning more about yourself in the process.

So, be the one that refreshes others' spirits with the empathy you provide.

7 WAYS TO CREATE GENUINE TRAITS

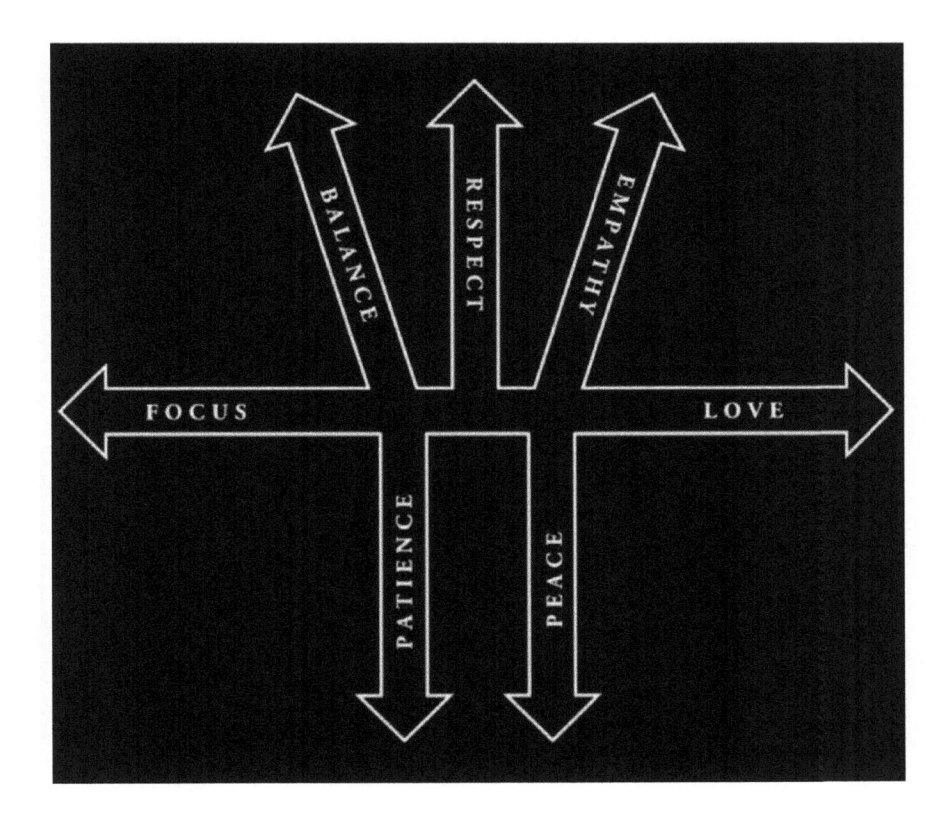

Diagram with arrows pointing in seven directions labeled: BALANCE, RESPECT, EMPATHY, FOCUS, LOVE, PATIENCE, PEACE.

Pick your direction and watch the success follow.